Infidelity

Tools and Exercises to Rebuild Your Relationship

(Proven Tips to Help Rebuild Your Relationship after Heartbreaking Cheating and Deception)

Clay Chase

Published By **Oliver Leish**

Clay Chase

Infidelity: Tools and Exercises to Rebuild Your Relationship (Proven Tips to Help Rebuild Your Relationship after Heartbreaking Cheating and Deception)

ISBN **978-1-998038-48-0**

No part of this guidebook shall be reproduced in any form without permission in writing from the publisher except in the case of brief quotations embodied in critical articles or reviews.

Legal & Disclaimer

The information contained in this book is not designed to replace or take the place of any form of medicine or professional medical advice. The information in this book has been provided for educational & entertainment purposes only.

The information contained in this book has been compiled from sources deemed reliable, and it is accurate to the best of the Author's knowledge; however, the Author cannot guarantee its accuracy and validity and cannot be held liable for any errors or omissions. Changes are periodically made to this book. You must consult your doctor or get professional medical advice before using any of the suggested remedies, techniques, or information in this book.

Table Of Contents

Chapter 1: Infidelity: Why Has It Happened to Us?

Is it possible to define the term "infidelity" in a relationship? In this case, spouses could face a problem. When we speak about infidelity, we are referring to sexual relations. True that sexual interactions are among the most damaging forms of adultery and cheating but there are different ways individuals become infidelity-prone in relationships as well as marriages. Cheating on your emotions involves becoming too intimate with someone else than your spouse, to the point where you cease to be interested in your principal relationship. The act of infidelity could be done either in person or online, but it is not accompanied by contact with sexual nature.

Certain actions we think of as minor could lead to significant act of infidelity. This is why it's vital to protect our relationship. Many couples are reluctant to discuss the issue of infidelity for a variety of reasons. For instance, during the early phases of a tie couples may be too romantic and therefore ignore the consequences of cheating and infidelity on their vows. In addition, couples may not bring the subject up due to the fear that one may interpret another to be untrustworthy.

Couples may tell one another that it is not acceptable to cheat, yet fail to explain the definition of cheating per se. Therefore, one individual may think that chatting with strangers is an excellent thing, while others find it unacceptable, and because there's no one-size-fits-all standard, couples could differ.

Typically, an act of infidelity is described as the breaking of an agreement to sexually engage among two persons within an intimate relationship. In the Romanticism concept, sex is not just an physical thing, but represents the most important symbol of love and the summation. Since the late 18th century the romanticism philosophy has been the human interpretation of love. Before the romanticism philosophy was introduced to the world, there were people who loved each other and even had sexual relations, however they were not aware of these two actions as sharing an underlying relationship. There was a possibility that people could have sex and not be in love, and others were able to enjoy but not be sexually intimate. The romantic philosophy puts sexual encounters as the ultimate expression of love, in which people express their affection for one another through physical sexual contact.

The romanticism beliefs turned infidelity into a catastrophe because it was impossible to separate the two from each

3

other. Also sexual activity was the result of a deep and intense desire to be committed to the person you love. It's difficult to conclude that sex was just a game between two persons. So, when we find out the fact that our spouse cheated on us with us, we associate emotions, feelings, and desires and the urge to make a commitment. We conclude that our partner is no more attracted to us and wants to live their lives together. The affection of our loved ones toward us has diminished. The assumption may not be right.

There are of course various instances in which being infidelity indicates that someone dislikes their relationship and is in search of another person; however, this isn't necessarily the case. In a few instances, it refers to something different. In some cases, it may be an unresolved feeling, an impulse to entice an erotica lover, or even a sense of elation that goes hand-in-hand with a sincere desire to a significant other.

Our society, culture, and education make it difficult for us to differentiate from love, and what we refer to as infidelity, and so it can be difficult to come over being cheated on. While some people are beyond the romanticism ethos and have been able to distinguish between deceit and love however, most people still adhere to belief that they are inextricably linked. This has turned into a problem that is of immense magnitude and impossible to distinguish the infidelity act from the individual. But, a spouse is spending time explaining an accomplice that their being infidelity was nothing but a joke and it is difficult to believe. Is it possible that sex, intimate conversations, or any kind of cheating have any significance other than all the other things?

We can conclude there may be an effective method to get out of the blockage. Perhaps, if we were to examine the thoughts of our minds as well as an honest recall of particular events in our lives We could find it simpler to distinguish love from infidelity, and thus heal rapidly. An honest examination of the mind could reveal that each individual is capable of some rather bizarre and shocking manner of loving one another and, at the same simultaneously, be entertaining or creating the perfect sexual situation in a relationship with another. The idea is unattainable when it is from the mouth of an unfaithful partner, who loves the other and engaging sexually.

In light of the concept of romanticism, it is possible to claim that it will be simpler to come back from the scars of romance if we do not focus on romanticism. If we can let go of thinking that cheating needs been a sign of beyond just an interest in physical intimacy and we could get a better chance of healing from these situations. Would it be better if we got rid of the mindset we use and look at various sources of information including our own personal experience? It is important to examine the mental patterns we have formed when the last time we thought about being in a relationship. The pain of being duped with will exist, but it's more easy to forgive and recognize the behavior of our loved ones. By putting yourself as your spouse can help you comprehend or accept the apology from our spouse. When we base our opinions of infidelity on our own memories, we might find it possible to soften redemptively to forgive, or even forget the events that happen as we are victims.

There are many questions to be answered: What is the cause of infidelity? And what causes us to feel in pain when being you are cheated on?

Infidelity is a reason for many reasons.

Why would anyone do something to ruin the relationship or marriage? This is a question that you should be asking yourself. If you've been a victim of infidelity you've contemplated a variety of inquiries. There are many consequences associated with the act of adultery and you'll be interested in knowing what led your spouse to cheat. There are a variety of reasons that go along to the numerous cases of infidelity and deceit. The evidence of adultery is different and is used for a specific reason. If you discover your spouse's status being in a relationship that is not legal, it could create a great deal of confusion for the. It could cause you to change your mind or end your relationship with a divorce. If you are aware of the reasons of infidelity, it is an initial step to improve the relationship you have after having an affair. The reason is that you'll know what is causing the issue and attempt to find an answer. The goal is to recognize the reason why people cheat. The following are the main causes for the infidelity

When You Feel the Relationship Is One-Sided

The biggest issue couples confront before they cheat is unbalance in their relationship. One-sided relationships may take on various forms, wherein one partner feels they're not appreciated and the other spouse feels that they're under more burdens on their finances than each other, for example. In the event that you feel you're more significant within a relationship than your spouse and you feel that it is a one-sided relationship, then that's unbalanced. If you feel so pressured by relationship, you might want to get relief from a different connection.

Lack of Enough Sex

There are many people who cheat due to not getting enough sexual sex in their homes. It is not just women only, but all people involved in the relationship. A woman or a man could decide to break up because of a lack appropriate sexual interactions. The study found that a majority of those who aren't satisfied in their relationships with sex tend to seek their fantasies fulfilled by people who they feel drawn to. Whoever doesn't enjoy an enjoyable sex experience has three times the chance to cheat on their relationships as opposed to people who are content. It also shows that 71 % of the men cheating were because of boredom with their sexuality compared to 49 % for females.

A sexy lifestyle that is loud can cause troubles in your relationship. There is a possibility that you are concerned about being infidelity due to the sex you have been living; therefore it is recommended to consider sexual therapy. Both you and your spouse are required to collaborate with a counselor to increase your marriage's intimacy and standing. There will be new methods for being together with your partner, as well as resolve any issues regarding your relationship, which had caused a negative impact on your sexual life.

Unfulfilled Sex Drive

It is a common excuse you've heard many times previously, such as "my sex drive is high for one partner to help me out or handle it." Most men would make the same thing, but women have strong sex drive, too. It is possible to have issues regarding sexual satisfaction in your relationship. fixing those issues can aid in keeping your relationship from falling into being in a relationship of infidelity. It is possible to have a thriving sexual activity, however you will have your spouse cheat against you. This is due to issues with their personal lives that need to disclose. There is no reason to cheat on your spouse because of a strong sexual drive. In fact, 46 percent of men and 19% of women who cheat have been accused of being cheaters because of this. There is a possibility that the sex you have been living is not fulfilling your desires. In these instances You should take advice with a counsellor and discuss about the best way to fulfill the desires of your heart.

Revenge for Past Activities

There is a chance that you don't want to believe it but a lot of couples cheat due to being previously cheated upon. In some cases, cheaters feel it's difficult to forgive the one who was cheating, and they might want to commit a crime in retaliation. It is a painful cycle which can cause greater pain than pleasure as it can cause an increase in the amount of infidelity. It is possible to work together with your partner if you suspect that you're likely to be cheating or if you'd like to enhance the relationship between you and your spouse by going to counsellors who can help in overcoming the issue and go on without a hitch.

Boredom

If you're bored you might be inclined to engage in an affair. Most of us are going through the same routines that include identical methods of conduct in your bedroom. It is important to find things that can maintain your relationship. Most divorces can be prevented in the event that people make space for one another and commit to regular communicating verbally in addition to physical communication that can bring enthusiasm. A lot of people seek thrills to keep from becoming bored which will be evident as they enter into new relationships, take up substances, or become involved with different individuals.

Most of the often, can result in a breach of arrangement between two parties and result in an unfavourable attitude towards relationships. The friendship of friends can create a relationship and develop over the passage of time, resulting in the possibility of a close relationship. Platonic friendship can turn into an affair when the relationship is intimate and also has a bit of privateness involved.

A break-up with your spouse could cause an infidelity. A lot of people feel not appreciated or valued, causing them to cheat their partners. The majority of these thoughts and secrets can result in doing things that aren't right and could cause regret later when the couple is in a relationship.

Chapter 2: Reaction to Infidelity - The Five Stages After the Discovery

Stage 1: Handling discovery

The first reaction that any person could feel should they find their partner doing something wrong is a sense of shock and anger. It is normal for a major fight to ensue along with lots of crying blame, explanation, and blaming. But, yelling at one other and not letting each other talk, or silently crying is not the best solution to deal with the issue of infidelity. How can one properly respond when they find the partner in a cheating relationship?

Keep calm This advice might appear unimportant to certain people, but it's among the main things is necessary to remember in dealing with an unhappy relationship. It is crucial since you will be able to think when you are calm. It will keep you and your partner from having to make an incident if you are able to recover your calm after noticing a shocking thing.

Confront your partner. The act of confronting your partner should not include entering the bedroom or throwing things around and shouting at him to ask his who the other is. Engaging with your partner is about asking honest questions from him. The confrontation must take place at a precise time, especially important if you are on your own. Engaging in a confrontation with your partner through screaming, punching or other aggressive methods will cause the other person fight back, and stop two from discussing things that are important to you. That's why it is important to face your partner with calmness.

Don't let the anger cloud your judgement - It's normal to feel angry when you find your partner being in a position of cheating, but who wouldn't? But, if you're trying to get things right, you should listen to and attempt to comprehend what your partner says. Permitting the anger of your partner to cloud your judgement and prevent you from understanding the thoughts of your partner won't be a good idea because being narrow-minded will make your relationship less effective.

Allow your partner to clarify one of the most important things you'll want to learn once you discover your spouse cheating is the motive behind it. Be aware that you won't know why you didn't allow your partner to explain the situation why they did it in the first place. Although it's an extremely wrong thing to do but your partner has the right to share. What's great about listening to others' explanations is that you'll be able to make decision-making more closely based on the comments of others as well as gain valuable life experiences throughout the process. Perhaps, for instance, you partner has cheated on your because you're not being honest about your conduct that he isn't able to stand and would rather search for an alternative. The argument may be painful however, in the end it will reveal why something went wrong and will help the decision to take to fix it.

Stage 2: Handling grief

There are five widely-known phases of grieving. It is important to understand is that the five phases could suggest that suffering is a linear process in which you progress between one point one level to the next without having to take a look back. It is my experience that grief is unique to everyone. The process isn't linear it's a process that can be different for everyone. You may go through the phases differently and have different stages or even repeat a few of the phases

Stage 1: Denial

"This isn't occurring to me. Maybe I'm dreaming." If you're having such thoughts, then it could be that you are experiencing denial. This is the initial stage. Similar to responses of those who've suffered other grievances, like the death of a loved one. The first reaction to the realization that your spouse may have not been faithful could be shock or in disbelief. When you suffer a physical injury it is a body's defense mechanism to protect you from the possibility of injury should the injury become unbearable. The same way that the organ becomes dull, so too does the heart of a human. It can be for either a brief or a long duration, based upon how long you require to shield yourself from emotional trauma. There is a possibility that you can recognize denial in your circumstance, and in the event that you don't, you might have witnessed it working in a person who you have met.

There was a belief that Hillary Clinton was in a condition of denial at the beginning phases of her relationship with Monica Lewinsky. The reality began to dawn after she was confronted by facts after facts and then in the form of a stained blue dress. The summons from Kenneth Starr to be a witness must have dealt an ominous blow against her reluctance.

The reason we deny is not a motive it is a subconscious procedure that shields us from extreme suffering.

Stage 2: Anger

If a spouse is offended, that spouse could be able to experience a massive outpouring frustration. If you're experiencing rage and resentment, know that this is a normal reaction after discovering that you are in love. In this moment, individuals yell and scream, while others swear to take to take revenge. In the end, the desire to take revenge can become overwhelming. At this point, when we witness women who throw their husband's clothes out of the house or donates his finest Armani suit to Goodwill. Another woman said that once her husband learned of the affair, he destroyed her teapot collection.

If you are able to acknowledge your feelings of anger and then express it safely, you're well getting started on the path to work through the pain. In the next chapter we'll go over this process more in depth and give you some techniques to deal with this overwhelming emotion.

Stage 3: Bargaining

As the anger subsides then the negotiations begin. As you begin to accept that your marriage is turmoil, you might begin to bargain. "I promise to be more considerate." "I'll be more loving." "I'll try to be better in bed." "I'll change my ways and be more attentive." At the negotiation stage it is possible that you are scared and numb to the idea about losing the love of your life that you're not able to think rationally.

Stage 4: Depression

The fourth phase is depression. There may be tears that flow. It is possible to feel depressed and become less interested in the external world. You may feel less hungry or you could feel like you are eating too much. It can be hard to concentrate. It is possible to become unfocused or be confused.

If you suffer from depression If you suffer from depression, you could be the person you would rather be. As an example, Diana was a princess. Diana was adamant about the infidelity of her husband through attempt to commit suicide, her bulimia and affairs with other women. Instead of seeking to take care of your self, you could be ignoring yourself or your appearance. Instead of seeking out pleasure and pleasure, you might be avoiding the idea. It's possible to think "If only I'd been more sexually responsive, he might not have strayed." "How could I have been such a blind fool?" It is possible to believe that you're in the wrong or you're not worthy of whatever happened. If you're experiencing similar symptoms or thoughts like sleeplessness and a lack of appetite or a lack of concentration or concentrate, a prescription from psychiatrists can ease the pain and allow your recovery to be more rapid.

When you discover the incident, it is possible to feel sorrow as date of the anniversary approaches. A lot of people are worried with the feelings of sadness that felt when they believed they were making progress and getting better. Through conversations with them it was often the case that their depression was due to approaching a birthday an anniversary of marriage, or even the date of investigation into the incident.

If you are experiencing an unresolved sadness, you could have an upcoming significant date. This can help you by understanding the root of your sadness is typically beneficial. But, it is possible to accomplish more through planning the activities you like and forming a support network in your direction.

Stage 5: Acceptance

The last stage, accepting is essential to move ahead. There are two types of receipts: the intellectual one, that is the first, and emotional, which occurs afterwards. The term "intelligent acceptance" refers to being aware of what's happened. Acceptance with love means that you are the one to talk about the infidelity of your spouse without having to go through being aroused by the reaction you had prior to the incident.

Remember that acceptance is the ultimate stage in grieving. If you're in the beginning stages, the final phase may seem impossible. Many people saying, "I can never accept what happened." Condemning being infidelity does not mean an equivalent to acceptance. Acceptance implies that you've acknowledged the fact that adultery took place. If you don't accept it, the consequences are sadness and the inability to be a believer to trust again. Most of the time once enough time has passed the majority of people are able to integrate both their emotional and intellectual acceptance of the loss.

If you've just realized that your spouse may have committed a crime, knowing the various stages of loss and grief will by itself not be enough to stop your pain. Be aware that grief can be different for individuals, ranging from a short to very long periods of duration. While infidelity may seem as if it's a funeral but it's actually a loss of all the dreams you in the beginning when you first wed. This isn't necessarily the end of your wedding as such.

Stage 3: Dealing with anger and anger

The most difficult part is because, no regardless of what you do it's impossible not to get angry at your partner. When someone asks whether you dislike someone then you're likely to be thinking about your boyfriend, girlfriend or spouse who was cheating with you. The resentment will not get any better. It will soon be difficult to tolerate all the activities you took part in. As an example, if you frequented a certain establishment every weekend, even though the relationship was still strong and stable, you'll start to avoid the same place after events turn to a halt. Similar to that, you'll find yourself hating all the things you loved in the past because it brings back memories of the past. It isn't a good indication, and it can hinder you from becoming content.

It's not simple to accept someone's apology after they changed your life and then left you all to fend for yourself. However, if you're looking to bring back happiness into your life, it is necessary to give up. Most of the time when a partner is cheating develops a strong dislike for the 'other' woman or the 'other. It's not a good idea and will not help anyone by any means. There are times when the third party may also be swindled because she's blissfully in a state of ignorance. Even if they're conscious, yet they have maintained an affair with your spouse but the reality is that it's impossible to change the situation. If you scream the lurgy of your soul or tear all the house down You can't alter what occurred. Instead of clinging the grudge and filling every day with negative thoughts, redirect your energies towards positive thinking.

If you continue to fill yourself with anger and frustration it will be impossible to capable of escaping the shackles of the memories. Imagine you are being held by a huge shark but you're unable to get yourself out since you are determined to hurt the shark, or even destroy it before you're able to be free. Would you consider this likely to happen? No. In fact, you'll be a victim of the shark because it is more powerful than you. In real life, too If you do not want to commit suicide, you must accept the past to let go of it. Relax hold your head up and keep moving forward.

Stage 4: Forgiveness

Humans make mistakes, but to forgive divine.

The saying goes.

We're not a two-dimensional creature living their lives in accordance with every maxim that we encounter. We choose our actions in order to see the possibility that lies behind them, not just for the reason that we've read about it in a fortune-telling cookie.

The same is true for us. we need to know what our future that we would like to make prior to allowing forgiveness for the person who has cheated on us. It is true that forgiveness is an absolute requirement - it's an essential part of the healing process, however how we define this is completely ours to decide. Do we wish to stay in a relationship? Are we willing to break apart but still be friends? Are we looking to end our relationship and not even think about one another?

You can take the various options in light of their merits however none is to be viewed by weighing negative feelings down.

The process of forgiveness isn't as straightforward to let our spouse free of the burden. This isn't necessarily to benefit their interests. you must keep in mind that giving them forgiveness is an act for our own good. It is impossible to find a tranquil inner peace when we hold on to our emotions, which force us to grumble or make us wake up during the late at night.

What we decide about our relationship moving forward should be done with a smile. This isn't just to stay clear of making decisions at the spur of the moment, which are regrettable in the future, but also to ensure that we are as separation from suffering as is possible. Sure, we'll definitely experience it for an extended period of time and will be able to feel it intensely. What we need to keep at heart is that it does not have to be a burden on us.

It is important to get rid of mental tethers as we move forward and take the maximum benefit from the new life we are able to. There is no way to rekindle our relationship with our spouse if we feel guilty for being in love with them. Nor will we be able to find a new partner by scrubbing every acquaintance we make and admire with the same risk of having an affair.

In fact, the decision to go out alone could feel like a perpetual pain when everything we do is always framed by the motive of being in a lonely place.

You must find our inner peace which is where we find our strength, and utilize it to remind us that while we are not required to be doing this, but that we could and would accomplish it as well. First and foremost, for ourselves as well as everyone else following.

5. Stage: To forgive and remain in the same place. Leave and forgive

Have you ever asked this to you? Are you prepared to view your spouse in a fresh way, or do ghosts of the past bother you? It's difficult to erase everything and go forward as though it was never happening. Whatever you desire, there's no button that could be shut off to allow us to erase the past.

Forgive and forget scenario can be a bit tricky because, despite what it is possible to forget your mistakes, you'll be forever reminiscing about the things your spouse was doing to you. When this happens forgiveness isn't helpful in moving on. Therefore, how do you determine if you'd like to accept forgiveness or not?

Let's suppose that your spouse was seeking forgiveness and sorry for what they did. They have sincerely admitted their mistakes and returned to you as they cherish you. What do you do in this circumstance? Only you can solution to this issue. Will you be able to forget the infidelity of your spouse and welcome the love of your life back? Do you feel the same love to them like you did in the past? If not, you might forgive them however, you'll never forget their actions. If this happens it is best to put the relationship on hold because it is impossible to repair the damage that was caused. If you do get back to your former partner There will be an obstacle between both of you. This could cause a tense scenario.

But there are times when you must ignore the offenders. A monotonous and boring life could make someone leave an affair. It doesn't mean that you should live with an unfaithful partner or be a victim of a toxic relationship. However, if your partner recognizes their mistake and then comes back to you and apologizes, consider allowing you and moving to the next stage in your lives. It could be anything related to your children's welfare to your personal feelings. Be sure to not make a judgment about the best and wrong option; just take a look at what you are looking for and what is important to you. It is best to take all the time you need to think about this issue. When you're sure you're sufficient to forgive your lover time, then go on to accept their apology.

Chapter 3: Moving On - How to Make Forward Progress

Accept the Changes

Your spouse has changed within their lives, and is now in a new relationship. Family and friends will discuss it and be supportive of you. Anyone that knows you will attempt to help them. However much you avoid meeting people from others, you need to face realities. This will be difficult to accept, especially in the case of marriage and had children. However, there's no solution to what transpired. Therefore, you must find every ounce of courage you can muster and acknowledge that you have changed your life.

The idea of change is that it can bring a new positive energy within your daily life. If it makes you feeling broken and depressed It is nearly impossible to take it on. The thoughts will be of those times you spent in a group and then have to return to your empty space and face all of the problems on your own. While it can feel like that your life is at an end You can make a difference by continuing to move forward and accepting your reality.

There are numerous ways that you are able to come out of the shadows after having experienced such emotions. Invite your pals to take them out for a movie night out with them. Enjoy time with your loved ones and talk about topics you're interested in. Take a book to read or dine out in your favourite eatery. Take a look at the things that you've always wanted to try but weren't able to do because you wanted to be with your spouse. As an example, suppose that you were a paraglider, but could not do it since your partner or girlfriend didn't like paragliding. This is your opportunity to try what you'd like to do. Try paragliding, and revel in the adrenaline-filled feeling. There is no need to ask permission from any person. It's yours to enjoy and have the right to live your life the same way as other people do.

Be aware that the constant change that happens throughout life. One way for us to be content and satisfied is to embrace the changes and continue to move forward in our lives.

What do you do now?

Two people are within this partnership, which means there are two individuals on who the relationship ultimately depended: Us together with them. Friends, family members colleagues, friends, etc. may hold different opinions, and different degrees of influence, however at the final analysis this influence will be exerted over the members of the relationships themselves which ultimately comes down to them if it will last or not.

It is possible that our relationships aren't working or even worse, through our partners or us. The issue isn't about delegating the blame, but it does have to do with the things we each want. As an example, even if we cheat with us, our spouse could be extremely regretful and would like to make amends by begging us to give it another chance, but they may not be feeling like that. If this happens we are the one to end the relationship.

It could be reversed.

However, it's essential to be aware of when this happens when it does, and in looking at the emotions of our own and our spouse's since ending your relationship may be just as difficult as solving it. It isn't an easy way to relief from stress unless the relationship was in a vacuum separated from all other relationships as we did not have acquaintances, they'd never seen our parents in person or lived within the same region or in the same area, and so on.

In turn, the greater our engagement to them, the more difficult to get them out of ourself from them.

We can however, and we will, if need be.

In the beginning, we must consider an aspect that is personal to us. have to take into consideration. What do we really want? The time is now to perform some deep-thinking after we've made an effort to get over the anger, and any other think-first emotions. We need to dig into our feelings to find out what we're doing.

In certain cases there are times when the pain is excessively deep and it might be that we forever connect with our loved one the bone-deep pain that will rob us of potential happiness if we decide to be with them forever as they smudge every single memories we make in a way that is unpalatable. The feeling is often similar to this when it first begins when we discover the truth, but it will become even more so throughout the years as we think over the implications and all possibilities and possibilities that are revealed. However, what should we do after it's been for months, which is a subjective time even after the sting of our fury have receded and we're still feeling that pain? This cursed, blasted pain.

It's not easy however, we've known that for a long time. The answer may seem easy, and yes, it's not easy.

The importance of time is in the timing. In addition to direct consequences The problem of making mistakes during the heat of the moment is because we don't take the time needed to become comfortable with your own choices.

The wrong timing to make long-term choices. Imagine packing and leaving the home, only to find you miss them so much and would like to return? This is certainly an alternative, but it must be framed with the correct perspective. This isn't a case of checkmating or the conclusion of the line, or anything like that. We are stopping for a moment and finding an alternative location to enjoy calm for a bit until we can get our heads back together.

That's why it is not advisable to make choices based on lasting outcomes because these permanent outcomes might be a repercussion at the rear of our heads with lasting results.

When we first begin in the beginning, we need to offer us options. We have the option of staying or go, and to updating or changing whenever we're at ease. Be aware that saying you are having a break doesn't necessarily require us to take only that. We can do more than. It's simple to determine if our vacation is an ongoing one which is why we're given the option of deciding that at all times. It is important to not creating more harm to the issue that we need to do, whether to the other person or to ourselves. We'll return to our topic.

The time has passed by in two months. It's almost gone but it is coming up in bursts and fits occasionally. The majority of us find ourselves feeling empty, struggling to determine how to proceed. There are many things that can occur in the span of two months, for instance, the partner deciding to leave the relationship by themselves. If that's the case maybe the best option we can take is to allow them to let them go.

It is important to note that there should be neither winners nor losers when it comes to this type of scenario no matter if the person we are with isn't mature enough to present it this way. If they are not want to be at their level, regardless of what the temptation. We're seeking the highest possible outcome. If this outcome occurs with no one who cheats against us and later abandon us, then so be it. You don't have to think that they received the outcome they desired, but we did not. That's the way things are.

Are they still around But what if they're still here? If they've not, to make the decision easier on us, to make that choice out of our control? If we don't have the information?

The most important thing is that it's still. It's still early regardless of arguments or embarrassing experiences, such as needing to tell the tale on a seventh occasion to a person who has just discovered - that have taken place in the past, they have maintained the sharp edges sharpened.

It might help to become to a more focused approach in this moment. This may sound like a flimsy approach, but it is possible to determine a time in which we put the issue in the context of our minds. We can say that we choose the 'grace' period that lasts between 6 and 8 months. It could be a great moment to go through all the motions and work together with our partner in working to improve the relationship. Work hard regardless of whether we're certain that our hearts are engaged at this point. Everything else should be natural after the initial numbness has gone away. It is possible to smile at the wonderful memories we've shared with each other, and feeling content in the fact that they're stepping back from fighting, and agreeing with us a lot more easily. We'll feel content that the relationships are working once again.

However, the reverse is also true. There could be more disputes, more refusals compromise, and an egregious repetition of the issues that were present, but with little or no any improvement. The time taken to take a look at the way the relationship is working can shed an unsettling light on the things we've never thought about prior to, or require us to face something that you've been not paying attention to. If a partner is in a relationship probationary period for their own faults must not make it more difficult to stay at peace with us at all, especially if they are looking to remain.

This is definitely not evidence that they are not worthy of staying on our side. When it comes to the grace period, being some distance from the first shocking revelation of infidelity could provide us with the clarity on the question of whether we are able to bless us with a greater portion of our life on Earth or not.

At the end of this time frame we aren't sure what we feel like, maybe this is in itself an answer.

And here we are in motion, but with them still firmly behind us. However, even though they're not firmly behind us. They're at our edges everywhere we travel. Although we've gotten ourselves out of the way, it's impossible to be able to free our families, friends and the natural world from.

There are still photos of people out having fun on social media. We are receiving invitations much less frequently to get together outings in which our ex-partner is there. It is difficult to keep in touch with those whom we believed we had a connection to. We blame it on the unavoidability of a breakup, and then try to tackle the situation each day by day and allow the injustice of it to pass.

However, it's not easy. We would like to be aloof and above all else, however, we're constantly on the brink of falling into tears. It is time to take another deep breath and a third one to cool ourselves you are around others.

We'd like to become better But it's overwhelming.

Naturally, going through everything is a challenge to our physical and mental endurance. Although facing the issue means you have to think about some of the most personal issues but we should be mindful of the fact that personal doesn't refer to being that we are all on our own. The majority of us have greater sources than we're conscious of. Stop, breathe, think. We must move on from our ex-lovers and those who could be behind in the separation, and toward people who will help us navigate through this.

Chapter 4: Trust - Rebuilding Takes Time

Do you have a way to prove your faith again?

For someone who has had a relationship ruined something, the situation is indecent and unacceptable. It is likely that you will be asking what happened, and even be blamed for the situation. It is possible that you believe that you're not enough and don't have the right to be appreciated. The pain will continue as memories of the hurtful experience will come at you when you don't make a move to heal. The only way to be able to forget about the trauma by allowing yourself to be healed, and you'll only be able save your relationship when you allow your self to forgive.

It is easier to come back from the hurt if you refrain from returning to your past. In the first place, it could bring old wounds to the surface; then it could cause miscommunication among you and your spouse. There was plenty of fighting when you first discovered the infidelity of your partner, and bringing back the memories from a long period of time could trigger these previous fights. In the end, you'll not ever be able take a single step to let it go when you continue to remind you of the events that occurred in the past. While it's a fact that shouldn't be forgotten, it is important to avoid bringing it up over and over again to create new memories to fill its spot. In the end, it'll be an opportunity for you to learn from your spouse and an error which should not be repeated in the foreseeable future.

A lesson you and your spouse have been taught, make sure to ensure that there is a constant flow of communication between both of you, as you've discovered how important communication can be in any relationship. Talk things out regardless of how difficult situations arise since it's through speaking with each other that you'll know what's causing the problem and the possible solution.

If you are looking to get better, don't be frightened. It can be an arduous decision to make, mostly since you've experienced the pain of being victimized, but it's something should be a goal when you are looking to make a change. It's not easy, but you have to learn to believe in your partner once more. Trust is earned, not handed out, therefore the best thing you can do is make sure you are willing to trust your spouse again. Allow him to grow and prove his worth. Don't be overly concerned of his conduct - trust that he won't repeat the same mistake and accept the word of his mouth as fact.

The process of letting go of an incredibly painful time within your own life can be challenging, but it's possible! It's just a matter of willpower and determination to persevere, and in the end, you'll be looking back on things that caused your pain, but which has helped you grow stronger and more savvy.

What can you do to win back the trust of your partner

This page is devoted to those who have committed a mistake by ignoring their spouse. It isn't an easy feat and you should be aware that it will be a long and difficult process. However, remember that this trip isn't without obstacles, and there'll come a time when you think of giving up. But what's most important is what you will get that will be rewarded at the end of the day, and that's a strengthened connection with your partner.

The first thing to do is if you want to restore your trust in your partner, the first thing you need to do is be fully accountable of your errors. Be careful not to say "I did it because you did this and that!" at your spouse, this will only make the situation even worse. Be aware that the decision to be in a relationship was only you, and the possibility of denying it was there and not done it, but you chose not to. But, consider this an opportunity to take responsibility and be honest your errors. Let your friend know you're deeply sorry about what you did and acknowledge the mistake you made.

When you've admitted your errors The next step is to acknowledge your mistakes and vow never to repeat the same mistake. Offer the most genuine apology you are able to come up with and be sure to keep every word of it. A mere excuse will not suffice. The most important part of an apology is the assurance that you won't make another mistake in the future. Your partner at first may be skeptical of the words you used, but if you prove to her that you truly meant your words and you're living up to the promise you made, it is likely that your spouse will be able to trust your word again. This will require a lot of effort, but so long as you've been true to every word you spoke, the hard work you put into it will produce positive outcomes.

One thing you should be aware of if you are looking to restore your relationship's confidence is to be totally open about your feelings the every time. Keep your feelings away from your spouse particularly if you are in a relationship. Falsifying your partner will not bring you anything good. If your spouse notices that you're truthful with her once again and she learns to trust you as well as gradually open and sharing her feelings with you. Be honest in your marriage which will eventually result in the restoration of confidence between your spouse and you.

Long-term relationships and love

A one that is damaged through hurt, betrayal and resentment is a challenge and demands a great deal of dedication, patience and commitment. The instances of infidelity within an intimate relationship is easily dismissed. This is one of the most devastating things that can happen to a couple. If both parties decide to resolve their disagreements and forget the hurt from the past and continue to work on their relationship and in the future, they'll strengthen their relationship by lessons learned from the time.

A long-lasting romantic relationship that is both rewarding and exhilarating for each of the partners after the union, is not an accident. This requires being aware of your desires, the things you would like to see in your relationship and communicating with your spouse with respect. You must be aware of what words or actions are hurtful to your feelings or anger you. Being loving again means paying attention to your partner's requirements and encouraging him let them be known. It also means being able to accept your partner for who they are, a flawed human being just like you.

Chapter 5: The Dos and Don'ts After Discovering Infidelity

Avoiding mistakes at all costs

First mistake: Do not discuss your spouse's relationship with your family or friends.

What?! Why don't you discuss the issue? Perhaps you're thinking why I'd give these kinds of suggestions from the beginning since we have been taught that discussing the issues we face will aid us. Even though that might be the case for some situations however, I would advise not to spill your heart about the infidelity of your partner when you're feeling a bit overwhelmed, angry and hurt.

Second error: Don't be rushed into making major important, life-altering choices right now

It is true that this suggestion might not work for all couples, contingent on your level of dedication to healing and the particulars of the particular situation. But for most couples, delaying any major life decisions you are considering by at least twelve months gives you the opportunity to get a better understanding on the matter even if you decide to break up with your partner later on.

Mistake #3: Demanding Explicit Details

You should not ask for specific information concerning the deceitful actions.

If you have recently discovered the sex abuse of your partner and you've discovered that it's nearly impossible to not ask for specific information because you must understand the severity of the partner's illness and even betrayal. There is an important distinction between aspects you should learn about and the situations which cause pain without justification. Keep in mind that once the facts are in your mind and you are aware of them, it's almost impossible to let them go. In the case of many partners and spouses of addicts who sex it is one of the toughest mistakes to stay clear of when confronting the emotional trauma that comes with betrayal.

Mistake #4: Failing to Set Boundaries

Be sure to draw sensible limits.

Boundaries govern the relationships. When you cross the boundaries of another, that you've violated the rules set by the rules. There is a variety of opinions about boundaries and limits for sexually addicted individuals. Some couples and spouses who are recovering consider boundary setting to be an effort to deflect control of the addicted. In certain cases it is. If you are creating boundaries that force an addict to reveal each and every action to you, or they have to face your consequences it is possible reconsider the reasons to set these limits. You are, of course, trying to keep yourself safe, which is acceptable and normal. However, are you making in an effort to control the person who is addicted by maintaining constant surveillance of the person? Healthy boundaries aim to ensure that there is honesty open between the two of. In particular the setting of a boundary which requires both of you to be honest with one another in all instances is typically better than setting a restriction which demands the person who is addicted to reveal his exact location each whenever he is out of the home.

Mistake #5: Pain Mining

It is not a good idea to torture yourself in the pursuit of discomfort.

The phrase "pain mining" does not define the very first memory of something painful, as sometimes the initial thoughts will suddenly come into your mind without warning. The process of mining pain begins when the first pain thoughts or recall. When the uncomfortable feeling is brought into your head it is a constant urge to indulge in pain mining since you're forced to leave all other things in your life in order to find something else that can bring you more emotional distress. The mind can wander through a painful thought before the next one, replaying things that your spouse told you every time inside your head. These thoughts lead you to imagine terrible scenario in your mind. thinking about your husband being involved in one or several of his deceitful actions. After you've been overwhelmed by the thought that is circulating within your mind and begin seeking evidence of deceitful activities in their personal computers or in their personal journals. It is a waste of time on end doing pain-mining.

Get ready for the pain The following 10 tips will assist in turning the page

1. Relational Trauma

Now it may seem as that the person who betrayed you took everything from you. The self-esteem you have most likely been broken. It is possible that you're having a myriad of emotions since your heart is broken. It is possible that you feel angry towards people they were in love who took your friend and love away from you. There is a possibility that you feel extremely grieving and may not be able to articulate the feelings you feel.

It is possible to feel anxious. There is a chance that you are scared of the future or scared over the current situation. What is going to happen to the children? Do I need to begin dating all over again, and do it all once more? If I don't believe any person any more? How did this happen? The simple fact that you don't know how to proceed or what's to come is a frightening thought.

It's crucial in this moment to understand exactly how difficult this situation will be for you. In terms of emotional impact, this can be comparable to post-traumatic stress disorders (PTSD) but this could be occurring in the present, and is also continuing to occur rather than being a recurring event in the past.

Health professionals and psychologists recommend that you seek the assistance that you require as quickly as you can is essential to ensure that you do not develop a chronic post-traumatic stress disorder, or to ensure that symptoms don't increase. These signs can become a part of your daily life, and then completely take over. With time, professional assistance, and taking good proper care of yourself, total recovery and tranquility are achievable.

2. Talk to Someone

In order to heal You will have to speak to someone. It can be difficult to find someone who whom you be confident in, someone who won't criticize your situation or you. It is possible that there are people who aren't your ideal friends for you to be talking with. This is the group of people who can make you feel tired and depressed after a conversations. They'll constantly give your opinion instead of taking in the conversation and engaging in healthy debates. They will be able to tell from the way you feel before and following the conversation. It is possible that they are not, and likely aren't seeking to cause you to believe that like this, but there are some who do not have the ability to converse or listening. It's a skill that must be developed as very few people "born with it."

It is your goal to meet those who are positive words to say for you and are open to hearing what you have to say. This is the group of people who assist you in answering the questions you have by offering their attention and encouraging you to take a path of thoughts that will lead you to your best solution. Conversations with these individuals are sure to leave you feeling confident and motivated You will find you are releasing a in a moment. The process will take time but it's important having someone you can chat with. Don't try to get through it all on your own.

3. Journaling

Journaling is an effective method for recovery. An investigation was carried out with three kinds of people were given different levels of depression. Each group was given an individual type of therapy. The three types comprised of psychotropic medication as well as journaling therapy.

Journalists were given the job to write for 10 minutes each day. The matter didn't matter how they wrote, they were simply instructed to write. They were instructed to write as if anyone would ever see the words they wrote. The writing could end up into the garbage or burnt once they'd written the piece.

After six months, chat therapy group was showing an improvement. The psychotropic medication group had returned to at the point they had started the previous six months. The group that journaled had the highest rate of healing and overcame depression at the speediest. The power of writing to heal can unleash is incomparable for many reasons.

If you ever are unable to finish the writing process and refusing to let yourself write the way you would like to think about the reason. Perhaps it's due to the fear that somebody could read what you've done? If so take the paper off your desk or burn it the paper after you're finished. Keep it in a lock and key. The most important thing is to not hold any reason to keep it.

4. Enjoy Nature

The use of nature to heal can be referred to as green therapy ecopsychology or ecotherapy. The treatment can be utilized for a variety of stressful and emotional issues and it has proven extremely beneficial for the majority of individuals. Numerous researchers around the world believe that a close connection to nature is beneficial for people's mental health and interactions with others. The idea is to get away from your desk or from the walls of your house is where you spend your time every day and spend time outdoors. It is the best way to build an emotional connection with your surroundings and yourself.

Psychologists suggest that when people discover this link to nature, they feel sensations of peace, harmony as well as timelessness and balance. A lot of people feel an overwhelming sense that something is bigger than them and out of their own self when they discover this connection, because they realize that they did not have anything in the making of these experiences. This requires them to acknowledge an underlying power that is crucial for healing process. This will be explored in the next chapter.

Nature is the thread that connects us all. All of us live on the beautiful planet. We often forget about our surroundings and the beauty of the world. A walk in the park or through the countryside can be a great way to heal. The beauty of nature helps us to put our lives into the right perspective. It can be easy to feel little when you look at the immense beauty of the natural world. Our pain are absorbed by allowing ourselves to take in the vastness of the natural world. I recall talking with an expert in wilderness survival once when he told me "In a wilderness survival situation, you find out that no matter who you are or how much money you make, nature does things her own way, she doesn't respect anyone." This is the truth about how irrelevant that we really are.

Nature lets us see the way in which life continues. Most of the time, following a loss or traumatizing event We would prefer the world to end for us to have some time to recover. But, unfortunately, the world does not end, and we tend to remain. This is similar to being in the middle of a river. that water (or the

71

universe) is constantly moving within us. If we're not moving forward, the world is moving all around us. There are a lot of opportunities to take from the natural world. Let me leave them for you to find out on your travels.

5. Find Something to Laugh at

It is the most effective medicine. It is said that French poet and writer Andre Breton said, "Humor is a method that permits one to brush truth sideways when it becomes too distressing." It is proven that it can reduce stress and anxiety. It's extremely helpful for helping patients with cancer cope through the constant pain and suffering of certain cancer treatments in addition. It is important to note that it can be used in a variety of ways for medical professionals which is why grief can be a discomfort. It is our job to help the pain disappear with a meaningful and real method. It's possible that you'll have a difficult time laughing in any way or smile. There is a sense of guilt because you feel joyful during this traumatic period or what might happen if you feel that happiness at this moment. You may have triggers that cause you to feel a sense of panic and remind you of an event before it happened. Some of the most hilarious movies and performers you've seen could be connected to memories that will not let you laugh. It's important to realize that there is nothing you should regret and there is every reason to experience joy and joy regardless of the circumstance.

Since so many of your memories could be based on things that such as the times you've seen amusement at times in the past, you'll likely have to search elsewhere to find something amusement. It is possible to start by reading the book that contains knock-knock jokes, even though you've never gone down this path of humor previously. It is important to seek out laughter. You are looking for something is what you're seeking. Set out of finding something that you can be jolly about. If you set this goal it is possible to find something that is funny.

The joy of laughing can free you. Did you know the expression "I laugh in the face of danger"? Imagine the meaning of being capable of chuckling when faced with risk. This is a genuine joyful laugh, not a panicked laugh. If you're able to smile when faced with risk, that means that you are able to put anxiety where it belongs, and have control over the situation. It's true that this is somewhat extreme and I'm not advising you to take on the lion, and then laugh at the fight. If you can be able to laugh in the face the sadness, despair, or fear What does it mean? This means that you do not regard anyone who has any influence over your life. This means that you allow them into your home when you wish them to into your home, but at any else time, they're subordinate to you. Sounds wonderful. The best thing about laughing is that it takes all else that is going on in our heads.

6. Self-Care

As life engulfs us and we're waiting for the ride, we can have an tendency to lose sight of the things which are the most important for us, the items that are most important to us. Sometimes, it's hard to determine which of these are. There are a variety of methods of determining the priorities you have however, often, the priorities we set aren't things that matter most. We don't take the important things the most as priority items.

Self-care can appear to be a selfish idea. It is possible to believe that you have more important things to attend to that the aspect of self-care can be put off until you're ready for it. Here's the issue: if we don't take the time for ourselves, we'll never have opportunity. It's unlikely to be the ideal time to take care of yourself. If you do not take care of what is most crucial self-care, then other aspects that you do in your life are going to be affected.

If you're a parent that need your attention, they're in good hands. It's difficult to find space to recover when you're rushing through life like the snowplow. It is imperative to make the time to be taking your own care, otherwise the other aspects of your life may be affected and may even get left unattended. As my mother used to declare, "you can either be in a position to be helped or a position to help another." If you aren't taking good care of yourself, you won't be in a position to aid others, not just your children.

7. Discover Who You Are

You're devastated. You're feeling as if you've lost certain characteristics. Your life (a large portion) is changed and forever altered. As your life has been altered, you necessity to discover the person you truly are. Certain people will help on this path, but ultimately, it's all entirely up to the creator and you. The process can take a while. This will cause you to take a look at yourself in the mirror and discover things you might not want to be However, this is a an aspect to the whole process. It is possible that you have no notion of who you are which is completely normal. Many people do not have the time to discover the person they really are. They stay in the shadows until their life has ended. Everybody has an elderly family member who says what they're thinking. They are at ease with their thoughts they don't think they need to be censors their thoughts because they understand the person they are and what they're worth. They are aware that no one other person's opinion of them will affect their perception of themselves.

8. Finding a Good Therapist

You received some excellent ways to begin recovering, however it's vital to seek out professional guidance when you have completed these steps. An experienced therapist will guide you and guide you through all the other steps that assist you in finding total healing and closure, so that you are able to live the most wonderful and beautiful life.

First thing to consider regarding this is that approximately 1/3 of all therapists will be detrimental and unhelpful to your needs. The remaining third of therapists will just be mediocre. It means that there's less than one-third of the those who are skilled and efficient. The same is true for every other field of work. Some tend to excel over other. Make use of the complimentary period they've given you to test the waters and determine the therapist you choose to be the right match to you. If you don't like the therapist, no matter what reason, you shouldn't worry about guilt. Look for a new counselor.

Many people will say "I have tried therapy. It was horrible. It was a nightmare." It means that you were treated by an "terrible" counselor who caused an unpleasant experience. Be sure to not let this stop you from seeking out a therapist. Utilize it to find a therapist who is compatible with you and your personal preferences. By working with the right therapy provider, the amount of duration it takes to recover will drastically decrease.

A lot of things get passed on through the word of mouth. This is the perfect method to get started looking into therapy providers. Find out what others have to say about each therapist particularly if they've had similar experiences to yours. They'll be honest with you on how they felt about their satisfactory or a bad experience as well as whether they would refer their therapist to you. Make sure to do your homework and make certain to spend the time finding the ideal person for your needs.

9. Your children: Keep this in your mind

It's a group of individuals that the traumas have caused us to suffer will affect possibly as much as they have affected our lives. It could be our children from an earlier relationship, or the children of our partner from previous relationships. Perhaps it's the children from us and our spouse.

Our kids will feel the brunt of this situation the most. No matter if we choose to remain with each other or not, in the beginning of this incident, without an adequate phrase, they'll see parents fight, argue and get angry. The environment in our home will be a bit tense as our kids will be the ones to suffer.

Whatever age or mature or robust they may be No child would like to watch their parents' relationships fall apart at the edges. We are two sides of their universe The fractures within our relationships can be just as destructive as the tremors of an earthquake. When we are hurt, they are often suffering as we do, even if they both are willing to avoid giving them those most painful specifics.

Keep in mind one important thing the fact that our partner is cheating against us doesn't mean they're an unfit parent. Who they cheated on the most is us. Even though our children are capable of making their own choices concerning their father but we shouldn't be a fool to think that they must cut the contact with their parents, or anything other than that.

This could be the way they would like to do, however, it is their decision. If we are able to encourage them or not is a matter to be made by determining if the partner we choose to work with is a great parent, whose presence can benefit our children - absolutely nothing else, and nothing less. It is also impossible to affect the thoughts of children that our partner has who were in a previous relationship other than if, of course, the partner we are with isn't an excellent parent.

If our kids aren't yet old enough to understand what's going on however they are aware enough to be aware of something happening Our main goal is to make sure that incidents affect them as minimally as is possible. When they are older and later on in their lives we are able to talk about it in greater detail when we'd like.

If we're married or even if we're not and feel that the children would be better being with us, then we should consult an attorney. No matter how bad like our spouse may be it is likely that they aren't going to give up on the children with no fight. Yes, there will be instances that our spouse may abandon the children and go away and leave, but chances are that they'll fight to protect their children. For that reason the same thing, it might be beneficial to seek out sole custody in writing even if the parent leaves on the whim of their own to avoid fighting over it later in the event that they alter their minds. It doesn't matter if it's because they love of their kids in a certain manner or they don't wish to "lose" or to make our lives more challenging it is possible that they will decide to take on the fight. When this occurs the best thing to do is contact an attorney and arrange to combat the situation. There's no reason it is acceptable to let a partner impact our children in any way other than we need to.

It is commonplace to give everything to our kids, but at times, this means being proactive and smart enough to seek out the right legal guidance when required. The majority of times an attorney for divorce could be able to assist in some way in this regard or guide us to the correct direction.

10. Save Your Relationship

The process of healing from the hurts of the past, and seeking to rebuild confidence in your relationship can be hard, but at time it's crucial the ability to preserve your relationship. However difficult things are, no one wants their relationship to come to an end. If you truly love your partner, you'll try everything you can to preserve the relationship.

Forgiveness is the key

If you've been cheated upon some people may suggest that you must forgive and everything will be okay however, you are aware you are more easily to do than it is said and there's no simple solution to be forgiven. But, they're correct. If you're looking to save your marriage and begin the next chapter in your lives You must be able to accept forgiveness. By forgiving, you cease thinking about how you can blame your partner for each and every thing is done, and get back to him. When you forgive, you allow yourself to forgive your past and demonstrate a desire to make a fresh start.

In the case of someone who has did a wrong by damaging their relationship for forgiveness, it is also an important factor. To whom do you need to be able to forgive? Yourself. When your relationship isn't going well and you are unable to stop yourself from continuing to blame yourself for your prior mistakes, instead of rescuing your relationship, you'll develop a sense of inferiority in the relationship. Being constantly weighed down by the burden of the past can lead to lower self-esteem, and you could allow your partner to think that you're "always right," even when it's not due to being scared to inflict more pain. It's not a good idea to have this relationship. That's why it's crucial to accept your mistakes - Yes, you did make an error, but it does not mean you cannot be able to make amends. You committed a mistake, however, that doesn't mean you have to be feeling guilty constantly regardless of whether it was the fault of you. Instead of dwelling on the guilt that comes from the mistake you made, consider learning lessons learned from the mistake. By doing this, you're not just making yourself more successful and a better person, you're also making a difference in the overall success of your relationship as an improved and better companion.

Collaboration is essential.

In order to save a relationship the effort has to be made by both parties. If one person only tries to maintain the relationship, chances of achieving success are extremely low. If two individuals are working together to bring back the love of their relationship, the situation could appear like nothing bad occurred.

In the event that you made an error, be able to keep the word you made. Be faithful to your commitments and remember to apologize and be sincere about it and be truthful. Avoid doing something that can cause your spouse to think or think that you're being suspicious. It was a long and difficult process to win her back trust. acting without thought will only cause your effort into a waste. Be aware of the way your spouse feels.

Chapter 6: Sexual Healing-Betrayal and Intimacy

Recovery of sexuality is essential following the event of infidelity. Sex is the most important aspect of relationships, and each couple must remain intimately and sexually linked. Moving from a state of complete disconnection (emotionally as well as sexually) following an affair can be difficult and perhaps impossible in a certain degree, and particularly if you're suffering. If you do decide to keep your relationship going you will need to ensure for you to collaborate in your sex relationship. It is an important element of the healing process.

Sexual health recovery encompasses every aspect of your life physical, emotional, as well as psychologically. Sexual intimacy should be considered in depth. In the meantime, until you have a way to get over the difficulties with your sexual relationship, the other partner within the relationship is likely to be sleeping with you on the inside. The connection between two of you might be too crowded, but there will be times when you desire to hold them by them again. It can be a method to recover and feel grounded and a reminder of the life was like prior to the affair. Couples could find the issues they are unable to share with the use of words are expressed by touching.

In the same way it can cause you to create walls that are high enough that you are able to defend yourself against all forms of vulnerability. It can take patience to love in like you have always done, however, be gentle. Don't pressure one another to get yet ready. There is a normal tendency to think about one another after an affair and think about what the sexual life of your partner is going to turn out.

There are times when you think that the volume of sexual activity you're having isn't enough. However, in other instances you may feel that you're putting too much effort into it. It is important to determine if this is actually good sex or if you're just trying to impress your partner. Engage your spouse in a conversation about the feelings you have. It is important to inform them regarding the possibility of having sexual relations. If you're not prepared let it be known loudly.

There are some facts you have to learn about sexual the following day after an incident of infidelity

1. The sexual experience is completely different thing after an infidelity. When a couple decides to remain together

following the other has been involved in an affair, it's the most important thing to do. Recovery isn't simple as this time period can be a test for every aspect of the relationship, not just sexual relations. Resuming a relationship in the bedroom is a great option for couples looking to reestablish their confidence. Sexual intimacy can bring on an array of feelings as well, so both spouses have be prepared for the very real consequences of relationships after an affair.

2. There won't be the same kind of relationship as you did prior to the breakup. If you want to make a move after an affair, it is important be aware that the previous relationship is over and isn't returning. At this point, you must focus on building relationships that are new including sexual relations. Be skeptical that you'll return to where you were. Your sexual relationship you

experienced in the beginning will probably have ended.

3. It is important to remain patience until trust returns. Sexual intimacy is a very intimate aspect of relationships that is characterized by high emotions. If you're recovering in which your emotions are extremely unstable and you are unable to remain with each other and not get angry, you should take things slowly. Allow the tension to ease before rushing to your bedroom.

4. If it is done in the right way and location, sex can be an excellent way to heal. It can bring couples physically and emotionally into places that words can't be. If you're at the right moment the right sex, and intimate time with each other can reconnect between you and your spouse.

5. It is necessary to change the priorities of your sexual life in a conscious manner. In the past, sexual activity was not an activity that required lots of energy. Perhaps it wasn't one of the most enjoyable times before affair, but it didn't require a lot of thinking or rethinking your priorities. But, you'll need be able to schedule sexual activity during your recovery conscious. Be aware that sex is an experience of healing in the aftermath of having an affair. Therefore, it is important be prepared start by becoming proficient at initiating the process, and then make the sex an absolute main priority. Be a bit adventurous on the bed if you need to be. It is important to demonstrate one another the part that sex will be in the new partnership.

6. It is necessary to lay everything out on the table including taboo topics. It's not

easy, however, deciding to leave involves repairing each aspect of your relationship. It is necessary to speak about sexual actions that led to an affair. If sexual relations were not as amazing in the past, it is time be able to admit it and search for ways to fix it. Take care of whatever causes a breach in confidence. Try to figure out the root of the problem. It may be difficult for you to come out initially due to the fear of hurting the other, but you'll need to open up. It is also necessary to discuss the events that occurred sexually during the relationship. Honesty is the key to be able to trust.

7. Be on the lookout for signs of dysfunction. Do you realize that a lot of individuals experience issues with their sexuality in the aftermath of having an relationship? If this happens to you in your relationship, you should not be afraid. Women may struggle to get

sexually enticed after an affair and men may not be able to attract an intimate erection. This is usually the case during periods of turmoil and stress. So, don't get caught up in the chaos. Take your time and take note of any challenges you could be confronting. If you experience performance issues or sexual relations triggers negative memories of that affair You may need to take a step back and allow longer to recover.

Nine steps to restore sexual intimacy

1. Don't compare yourself to your lover in love.

Each person is unique. Therefore, the idea of comparing ourselves with others is not a good idea on any level. Like flowers, we are shades; we are all unique, beautiful, and individual. If you say the color of one is superior over one is to make a mistake. Beauty comes from diversity. If we were to say blue was prettier than red, we would do not remove the hue. The world would be in complete peril. There are positives and negatives in anything. There are both good and bad aspects for all. So, trying to prove yourself through pointing out weaknesses in other people or vice versa could result in failure. It is possible to be better than someone else than you, more intelligent, funnier and more attractive etc. Even though the super sex born from competition or jealousy can be amazing but it must shift from being selfish and to be the base of love, trust, and security within the relationships. It should focus on understanding how much you're valued, admired and appreciated by your spouse.

The best sex should focus on you and not your competition. If you remain with self-focused sex this will result in failing in the end. A comparison could result in a feeling of repulsion. A betrayed spouse might resent the notion of his partner having sexual relations with someone other than herself so badly that she doesn't want any kind of intimate relationships. Your spouse may have the capacity to forgive however, if the idea of sexual intimacy is raised it is not a good idea to pursue the subject.

2. Be free of the feeling of guilt, shame and unworthiness.

In some cases, the failure to restore intimacy may be a result of those who have cheated. In the above example one could suffer due to regret and guilt over the fact that they can't get sexual fully. There are some who find sexual arousal difficult because they haven't completed the relationship or aren't sure in deciding whether they should continue or end the relationship. Some people, however, aren't happy with the woman they had a sexual relationship with, and therefore they have difficulty engaging the person who was their main partner. It's normal and it may take some period of time before they are deeply sexually sexy again. There's a lot of loss and grief taking in these moments and both partners must be able to move past the escalating drama. In the event that a cheating spouse mourns over the loss of their lover, it's not about who they are however, it is about the feelings of being in an affair. In the course of their relationship, an cheating spouse believes that he has fallen in love. And really, they're amazed by how romantic it can feel. Being beloved and loved by an outsider is appealing to the individual. The issue of intimacy isn't simple to deal with after an affair They can be just as complex as the rest of life. Don't look at a one-size-fits-all solution.

3. Following an incident, it is important to rekindle the connection is all about us, not him/her.

The majority of individuals, particularly those who have been cheated tend to seek out the blame. They believe that the person who did wrong must repair the relationships. One spouse may be thinking that because they both been a failure in one manner or another the onus is now on them to mend the rifts. The couple must realize that their relationship is centered around the two of them, not only either one of them. It is important to avoid saying "he has an issue" or "she is the problem." It's about two people. Healing should be a "we" thing.

The spouses need to understand the significance of sexual intimacy and sex when the process of repairing a relationship following infidelity. It involves the healing process, reconciling following disagreements, helping the other person, gaining confidence in themselves, showing affection in a more profound and greater way when the words do not work, reuniting with a greater degree of intimacy and arousing each other and also feeling beautiful.

4. Don't force anything.

Following an affair, affection can aid the couple to heal. The earlier it takes place more quickly, the more beneficial. But, nobody should make the other feel the desire to have a sex session. It might be present, but try to not push or hurt one another. Therapists may suggest that couples should be patient before becoming sexually intimate. But both partners must be in touch in the earliest time possible.

5. Don't interpret sexual intimacy as an indication of complete reconciliation.

Even though sexual relationships are an integral one of the steps in reconciliation The partners (especially those who are the perpetrators) must not think that everything is in order. There are many things that need to happen before the marriage can heal to the fullest extent. Reconciliation takes the time, patience, and openness along with a myriad of other qualities. Be aware that complete accord could be a challenge in the event that the couple holds their sex aside for longer than is necessary.

6. Find out how you can converse truthfully and freely with your partner.

Couples need to know the ways to talk about sexual encounters in a non-judgmental manner without making assumptions about the other. Talking about your secret desires and learning the opinions of your partner is acceptable. But, you should not discuss concerns about intimacy during intimate. Pick a specific time when you can talk about the issue. If you are sexually involved and the relationship doesn't seem to go according to plan such as if there is a problem with one of you Do not be pushed. Keep your hands together and let the tension is gone. Do not discuss what transpired in the present and then wait for a suitable moment to join with the conversation. Set aside sex time between the moments you engage in conversations about sexuality.

7. Try to calm your sex as you recover from the being in love.

In general, there are two kinds of the sex you can choose from: wild, romantic erotica and lovemaking sexual sex. Both are acceptable for marriage or in a relationship. But, the time to heal needs gentle and comforting sexual relations. As you work to rebuild the trust of your partner, the sex you have to engage in should be one of lovemaking.

8. Recover the hearts that have been broken to restore the love.

Rebuilding sexual intimacy after the cheating incident requires kindness, patience and a sense of understanding. It is important to realize that sexual therapy is not possible without marital therapy. Both treatments must cooperate. Every marriage and relationship couples need to mirror one their partner. The wedding's theme is reflected in the private events and in reverse. So, you need the ability to heal your hearts and achieve the perfect sexual intimacy.

9. You must be willing to indulge in the dreams of your spouse (within boundaries).

If your spouse was cheating due to feeling unsatisfied with the relationship, you have be aware of the issues that were met by the cheating and then be prepared to resolve these. To rebuild the relationship the cheater needs to pay attention to the demands of the victim in returning the confidence that they are attracted to sexuality. If a person commits certain actions in an affair and is willing to perform them within the main relationship as that the spouse who was betrayed has the desire and is willing to do it. One excellent illustration of what could take place in a marriage is the possibility of having sexual relations in a car. Both spouses must be willing to experiment with this in the relationship. It is possible that the bed will be comfy, but if the spouse would like to experience the excitement in the car, then you should be prepared to take a risk.

Be aware it is a love act that isn't solely about you. Therefore, if you're cheating, and tried to do something during the marriage that you're not willing to commit in the wedding, then there is something that requires to be resolved. It is important to determine what is the issue. This could be guilt, shame, depression or something else. Perhaps it's the manner in which your spouse kisses you or how clean he is? Keep your mouth shut, be honest and use dissuasion. One thing that you can be certain of is that marriage with no intimacy will be a failure. So, any problems regarding infidelity need to be dealt with immediately.

Chapter 7: Seeking Help

We discovered that we were being cheated our credit card, it was like that the entire world had crashed into us, an overwhelming shock, and the sound was inaudible and envelops itself in our ears.

In accordance with our personalities and the context of how we were exposed the information, our responses may vary from one person to another. However, in the end everyone looked for assistance elsewhere and that's even if the help comes as a helpful and sympathetic publication.

It is applicable to all aspects of the relationship after the revelation of infidelity. The advice that we solicit isn't unavoidable; it is just too much of a burden to put upon anyone. But, you do need to be truthful and impartial. Even people with opinions (I am not a fan of your husband) could be an immense assistance if they're honest both with themselves and you about their prejudices (I am not happy with your husband however, if you're determined to succeed I'll be honest with you and help you in any way I could. I'm not going to start a an ignition source for his vehicle).

Just had one carpet taken away from us. There's no need to depend upon someone else's unreliable. Be aware that while this issue isn't likely to be to the severity of our partners behaviors, it may potentially have devastating practical implications. Consider, for instance about the consequences of expressing our most painful feelings in front of someone only to see our friend confront us by blows similar to. It's possible that they have decent intentions, but remember that the way to hell is lined with good intentions also, so follow this suggestion and keep the way from those who behave such as that.

Family is often the most thorny of enemies when it comes to it comes to support. There are times when we'll have people who are angry on our behalf however, it's refreshing to know that they are always in our corner. But it is possible to encounter people who will use the occasion to tweet a badly punctuated I-told you-so, or even criticize us, or even use us as a source to spread gossip. For clarity, friends and acquaintances could perform the same thing. The problem is that it tends to be an even harder when the family has a responsibility. It is important to be cautious and remember that just because they are family members doesn't mean people less humans.

They're as compassionate as anyone else however, they can also be just as brutal.

In the present, let's suppose we've been through all of our familial and social circle of friends to find people we can trust. However, that doesn't mean there's no one we can count on. We may have been relying on them for a prolonged period and are worried about rubbing off their trust or maybe just not making use of their great quality of life. There's also the possibility that they're a bit closely associated with us and our spouse, which makes difficult to find any opinion that we can rely on regardless of whether it's objective or not.

The answer, obviously is to get aid from strangers.

It's not that you should go out our doors at the crack of dawn to check the first jogger sporting the most tiny dog we spot -- but this is not a stranger. You should go on a hunt inside that vast void of fantasies and delusions that is also called the Internet. Remember that the internet universe is in fact an expression of human nature as a whole, therefore be careful in the same way.

It is possible to dip our toes into Google to find out the best way to deal with someone who is who is cheating on you. The results may differ depending upon the place where the user is located and how the search was initiated and, generally, we will receive information from many sources, from psychology studies, magazines and blogs.

Truthfully speaking, those reports based on research into psychology tend to be the most reliable when searching for information and stats. As an example Google search for five minutes might lead us to information that someone who had cheated in one partnership is 3 times as likely be a cheater in the next. If we're the next one', it could make us feel more compelled to get it done now, and move off as well as we possibly can. The power of knowledge is in the hands of experience with a bit of experience could be a big help to help in the event of a crisis.

Here are a few more suggestions You should use multiple websites. It's always beneficial to find out which experts aren't in agreement on, as well as which areas they are more in agreement on since this can be a sign that the information they provide is reliable. Also, be aware of sites that claim to be professional sources. There's no single source 3 easy steps do-it-yourself methods to deal with our emotions that have been accumulating over us. Just like everything else worth doing you have to put in the work and have done it correctly.

It is also possible to come across somebody telling us how we can cut our ex-partner's tire and then allegedly be able to escape the consequences. Most likely, there will be a few suspect parties that will encourage even more extreme ways of retribution. Avoid doing that. They are crimes and it's not a good idea to forget that we'd probably be the prime person to be the victim following the breakup.

Also, it's wrong. When asked about this, make sure to mention it before you answer!

However, that doesn't mean blogs and magazines don't play a role in the debate about post-cheating. professional-sourced content is notable due to their objectivity and facts-based reasoning, but they also can come off as boring reading material. Understanding facts and figures is already challenging enough without adding more stress or grief to the process. An honest blog article or an article by a skilled journalist who is looking after their readers may be a great way to help us get back on track or at least help to boost our spirits.

Of course it isn't a good idea to ignore forums and online support groups. There are numerous online forums that allow us to log on anonymously, vent our anger and chat with other people going through the same struggles as we do. These sites can prove to be an ideal refuge for number of motives. First of all, as long as our username isn't "FirstNameLastNameBirthday," there is anonymity. Nobody will be able to tell what we're about and everything you say is connected to our identity. This can be an excellent method to let our emotions out. Second, online support forums and forums are full of those who have experienced or are currently in something similar to us that are able to empathize, relate and be there for our needs. You must ensure we choose a reliable support group or we don't accidentally join into a support forum for something completely different. It might be difficult to appreciate the benefits of these communities on the internet initially, but only you will soon be able to judge if they're worth the investment. The third reason is that the web doesn't offer hours of operation. It doesn't matter if it's the night or at the break of dawn, you can access the internet and chat with anyone. It's not always immediately, but there's unquestionably therapeutic benefits in having a space to express anger or worry, or even frustration without bottled up.

Even studying about animals with fuzzy fur will help. What works, will work. Do not dismiss it because it's not conventional. Look for a solution wherever you can, as the expression is.

If that's not something you've heard, it ought to be.

There are also plenty of video websites to serve this function that range from the professional to the amateur. If sat back, absorbing the thoughts of others is what we prefer to do is a good alternative too.

However, what happens if all of this doesn't work? We've watched countless minutes of Top 10 Ways to Get Over Him videos, and we're as down and crushed as when we first started. We've completed a variety of Is He A

DoucheBag quizzes on the most popular dating websites or maybe, even to a survey on Facebook to determine how many women have walked off of their partner's lives. We've read an article upon article that is which are based upon real-life research trying to follow the tips the articles provided for calming a troubled soul. We've had conversations with strangers over the web and received their tips.

There's nothing new, however. The feeling is still like the chest is a hole And now, our family members are concerned about how we've been off work for the entire week. Concerning our inability to eat. Our self-imposed isolation from social occasions.

This, along with other signs indicate that everything seems to be not right It is unlikely that we will be improving without significant assistance. Sure, our relatives and friends gathered to support us may be helpful however, there is no alternative to a person who has specifically trained to assist those in this exact situation. There is no way to avoid the situation.

Let's take one thing out from our way. The fact that we have to visit a doctor isn't a sign of weakness. Everyone has different requirements which is why it is sensible to take advantage of the many resources is available to us.

Let's try it again. There is nothing to hide from when we seek help.

Nothing.

Couples therapy may seem as a major step however, in our situation there is a bit that has some silver lining. The reason we are hesitant to attend therapy together tends to be based on acknowledging to ourselves that there is something wrong. Well. It's a matter of infidelity. The situation isn't quite to that point at which we're wondering whether or not we're blowing things way over the top. If none of the other options are working at all, and arguments are still rolling into the room, or if communication is slowing down and couples therapy might be just what we need for getting things moving in the right direction. Have you thought about the importance of having an objective opinion before? There is no opinion that are more objective than those of one from a qualified medical professional.

One of the biggest issues when a spouse cheats against us isn't the cheating the act itself. It's not that our spouse was involved with someone else which bothers us. It's an act of betrayal. This has been discussed in the previous chapters. This painful loss of faith is the most difficult piece in the majority of cases.

Note that visiting a marital therapist psychologist does not assurance that we will be able to save our marriage. But, if approached properly by a therapist, it could help us take substantial efforts towards this final goal. As previously mentioned it's only a possibility if we are looking to save our relationships.

If we're able to stay together and not support of an experienced professional could assist in healing our wounds as well as defuse anger. enable us to get over the incident.

An additional note is that mileage can be different from therapist-therapist. Be sure choosing a therapist both of us feel comfortable with. There are also distinctions between psychologists, psychiatrists and others. They are more geared towards the medicinal aspect that isn't the best option for those who are taking a dip into counseling. Look up the kind of doctor that is needed. They will declare themselves to be counselors for couples if this is what they specialize in.

It also has the undisputed benefit of privacy. There is no need to think what we discuss do not ever go away just like be confiding with family members. While we may love and trust them, anxiety is never far away even if it doesn't disappear completely, even when a therapist has a moral and legal obligation to protect our private thoughts private however, it's likely that they will be more discreet.

If this doesn't sound like enough, keep in mind that we've been aiming to the best-case strategy since the whole affair began. We'd like to live in a world where we and our partners wouldn't have done the things they did. however, here we are doing the possible. Sometimes, we require professional assistance. What works, does the job.

After all that it is possible that we will have solutions to the burning concerns and questions however, we should not be dissatisfied when we don't. The benefit of seeking aid is that it's often sufficient for a sense of security when you're in stress. The feeling of support is valuable by itself even though it may appear to be rather useless. It's about our mental health since we're all in this together.

There is another positive aspect. We have a source that we can draw from as we come together in order to confront everything that occurs as a result from our partner's conduct. No matter what There's always something more needs to be dealt with.

Chapter 8: Infidelity in Marriage

The breakup of a marriage can be caused by infidelity. of the best relationship. There are emotions of anger, betrayal and guilt. Although there are additional marital issues (money problems as well as health problems, disagreements) which husbands and wives are forced to deal with and deal with, infidelity is a major blow to the base of union. This is that many marriages end ending in divorce or divorce. But, there are also couples who can overcome the issue of infidelity and repair their relationship.

Infidelity Defined

Infidelity isn't a one-size fits all well-defined situation. The definition of infidelity varies between married couples. There are diverse ways that you can define and view relationship infidelity.

How can you define the emotional bond that is formed between two individuals? Can it be considered to be an act of infidelity even if there's not physical contact? What do you think of the modern trend of online relationships? Is a couple who is engaged in an online affair be thought to be guilty of to infidelity?

Do you think that these relationships are mainly fantasies? those who are not part of the relationship is frequently considered to be a way of escape from real life problems?

Why Do Affairs Happen?

The motives behind the reasons for affairs are discussed in this article. There are a myriad of factors which contribute to the infidelity and cheating. A few of these causes don't have anything to do with sexuality. A few of them stem from personal issues like lower self-esteem, addiction to sexual as well as alcoholism and addiction to drugs. Marriage issues that have been in the background for quite a long time could also be the cause of the desire to have an relationship.

The partner who is having an affair typically:

• Feels a sexual desire towards an individual other than or her companion. If the person decides to take action on the sensation instead of denying it, then the person begins to be a liar.

* Ensures that the matter is kept with absolute secrecy, through deceit and lying.

• Talks with a person different from their spouse regarding the problems within their relationship.

Feels a stronger emotional bond with a sexual and romantic relationship with someone else than their partner.

* Conjures up unrealistic fantasies about an individual other than or their spouse.

Cause and Effect

There are many reasons people may have an affair that is not related to the marriage. This could be an issue of poor judgment. The husband may feel content in his relationship however a night out at the office with the occasional drink can cause a lack of control.

Certain married couples seek feelings of connection because the spouse they have been with hasn't paid attention to their desires or they feel less attractive to their partner and so search for approval in other places.

No matter the motive behind the reason for someone to engage in an affair The consequences of infidelity within a marriage can be catastrophic.

Chapter 9: Unexpected facts about cheating

This article will help you uncover some facts that you didn't know about being in a relationship that is not working. The information provided in this article could assist in preserving your wedding.

Do you know when to tell if you have an unfaithful husband? Can you identify when a wife has been not faithful? Many people believe that if one cheats in relationship, it means that he has a problem with his partner. This isn't always however. If you talk to self-confessed cheaters to reveal their cheating habits, they'll inform you about their happy marriages in the wake of their indiscretions. They state that they're typically content with the relationships they're getting from their spouse and don't really look for an escape route. If this is true then why are some guys (even women) find themselves in bed with someone apart from their spouse?

These details will tell the way in which it happens:

1. The majority of husbands love their wives even when they are guilty of infidelity.

Many men who have an affair with a woman haven't necessarily lost the love for their wives. they are just unhappy with the present status of their relationship. The most common reason for affairs is as a couple enters an "companionate love" phase in their union. It means they've got settled and have children, and they have managed to build a solid foundation for their lives.

It appears that they have built an enduring foundation for their relationship. The husband can manage to support the family, and the wife has developed into a competent housekeeper, love is often lacking in their relationships. The issue is often exaggerated in the event that couples do not discuss their issues with each other.

A majority of couples, instead of having a discussion about specific issues within their relationship, choose to remain silent. They start to search at the areas that they feel are not being addressed in their relationship with an individual.

2. Men generally commit a sexy act with women that they already know.

Cheaters aren't required to pick an unintentional girl at a bar or in coffee shops. A majority of relationships are the result of a friendship. The constant bonding that triggers relationships in the majority of men. A lot of women believe that cheating ladies are floating. However, they're certainly not. These are typically women who have a good education and have lucrative jobs and are well appearance.

They are more likely to feel connected with women who are not their wives. They may have a friends for a long time or a coworker.

3. Many men cheat in order to keep their unions.

Do you think that the majority of men who commit adultery have a love for their wives yet do not know how to resolve the marital issues, so looking outside the marriage in search of an individual to fill the gaps? They aren't looking to divorce their spouses, but they realize that their relationship is in troublesome issue, but they aren't willing to face the problems. They end up "living happily ever after" with their wives as well as their lover, but without confronting the issues that are causing problems in their relationship.

4. The men hate themselves for cheating.

Many people believe that cheaters do not have morals, some are inclined to resent the actions they took following their blunders. People who put aside their pride will be remorseful for committing a crime against someone they love. Many cheaters are viewed as failed people after cheating on their wives.

5. Cheaters are often sexually physically.

The men who start to cheat are more sexually desire. Once his sexual desire is activated, it's with his wife where the most sexually comfortable he feels.

6. Women cheat, too.

If women are cheating, they tend to engage in more "dangerous" affairs. Women and men cheat on each other for various motives. The majority of women cheat because they seek sexual satisfaction. However, for them, the sex aspect is not the primary reason. Today, a growing trend is relationships online and experts believe this is the most harmful kind of infidelity. The type of relationship that is much more focused on the emotional aspect and females are more likely to choose the type of relationship. If a relationship is only focused on sexual intimacy, it's unlikely to last as it is not as emotional.

7. It is common for wives to know she is being cheated on by her husband.

The majority of wives realize that their husbands cheat but they are unable to bring themselves to admit the fact. The majority of wives are unaware that these cheating occurs. They are often unable to endure the shame and aftermath. They are unsure of the future they will have and are worried about the possibility that if they tell their spouses know that they know about the cheating, they'll be abandoned.

8. Couples who are married cannot be able to work together when the husband is involved in an affair.

Couples can choose to decide to work things out however it doesn't matter so long as the husband remains involved in an affair. So long as the husband's still in love by the girl who is currently the apple of his attention and no efforts from his wife will stop him from getting off the hook. The husband believes all is well with him, and would not want to ruin things by introducing his girlfriend to a new one. In reality, it is his decision if and when the relationship will end up falling to pieces. If he isn't aware that his life can never improve with his lover there is nothing that can keep their relationship from falling apart.

9. The marriage is often ruined by affairs.

It's not as difficult as it seems it is possible to help save a marriage. Hot and new relationships can be thrilling, but they may also ignite a relationship. As husbands start to see that their relationships aren't so perfect as they believed, they may decide to stop the relationship and begin a new love affair with wives.

10. However, even after they repair the marriage, spouses will not be able to forget having an affair.

It's a sad reality although even if a husband decides to save the marriage, he'll never completely forget the woman whom he had an affair. There is a chance that he'll miss the fun of his other woman, and often be unable to remember how it affected him. Men tend to continue with their lives because they believe they have the control. They usually gain confidence back in themselves because women still find their appearance attractive.

The familiarity of a marriage can lead to boredom. Even after the marriage is restored, some couples can't swear to their weddings.

11. An unfaithful spouse or husband is aware that she or he has hurt their loved ones and also their families.

The partner who has been cheating might find it difficult to accept the affair, but still carry into the act. If he senses that he's unimportant or not appreciated He will seek out an individual who will give him the respect he requires.

12. It is wrong to hold wives accountable for the indiscretions of their husbands.

If a husband is not faithful He is at his own decision. His wife is not in any way to have anything to do with it. A common reason for husbands they believe their wives forced them to the arms an other woman is a complete falsehood. They are the ones who cheat and they knew that they committed the act.

Chapter 10: The Reason People Cheat: Differentialities between Women and Men

There's no gender which is more prone to cheating than any other gender in a relationships. The practice of cheating is more widespread than many people think. Although the majority of people know that infidelity between spouses is not correct, it is still common to see spouses or husbands in a relationship who is cheating on their spouse from time to time.

Here's a short list of distinctions between women and men in the area of cheating:

The majority of women believe that it's wrong to be in love.

Through surveys and research by women, the majority of them agree that cheating or infidelity, especially after being married is untrue. Although there are some women who believe it is unjust, they do continue to do it to their husbands as well as some cheat with another husband. Men may think it's a wrong action, but they do it. The majority of the time the men are operating under an unbalanced view that it's acceptable to do it, however it's unacceptable when it's their wives that cheat.

* Men are more inclined to be cheaters than women.

Men are more likely to engage in sexual relations with a woman in the marriage. It is common for married men to go on one-night-stands, however some husbands have an ongoing relationship with another woman. Women with less experience are more likely to spend time with males other that their spouse while they are being married. However, there are also women who'll enter an affair with someone apart from their husbands, for the security of their relationship and to build emotional bonds.

* Women are more free in the present and tend to cheat more than they did in the past.

This generation of women tends to be more susceptible to cheating than the women of the not too distant times. With increasing numbers of women are employed They are exposed to other individuals and, in particular, when their careers involve them traveling. If you take a look at women of the past 20 years and you'll notice that the vast majority are content with looking after their home as well as their families. Hence it is much less likely to cheat.

Nowadays, women are able to do what men would be able to do, even cheating.

Cheating does not have to be all about sexual pleasure.

It's not easy to imagine, cheating isn't only about sexuality, and it's true in the case of a large portion of males. When you inquire about males (though they will not admit they cheat themselves) They will tell you that they cheat due to an unease from their partners and discover the love they're seeking in a different. Some cheat on their wives because they tend to be more focused in being moms and homemaker, and they don't realize that they are the wife of their spouses.

Women and men who commit adultery seek to be loved by their spouses. When they're not, they search for that outside of their relationship. It is the same for most women. They have the desire to commit cheating due to the feeling that they're getting a bad rap from their spouses, or because they aren't feeling beautiful enough and that's the reason they want the approval of others, before they commit a crime.

Cheating isn't only about appearances

There's a good chance you'll be shocked to learn that the vast majority of people who have cheated didn't in a relationship with a person who was better-looking or healthier than their partners. This may also be a an unexpected fact that people who do not cheat tend to be more beautiful.

The cheaters don't have to be honest that they've cheated.

The majority of men, as well as females, will not be accused of cheating on their spouses regardless of the evidence that would suggest contrary.

* Males tend to be more willing to accept cheating wives.

It's shocking to learn that males tend to be more willing to accept the forgiveness of cheating spouses. However women tend to be less forgiving. However, there are some who are willing to be willing to forgive their husbands in order to preserve their union. However, it could differ in the event that a woman gets pregnant by a man, but.

The majority of cheaters weren't really unhappy about their relationships.

The men who have been cheated on at one time or another didn't be in a bad relationship. There are a handful of people who would declare that they're having a bad marriage. The majority of men are married to "happy marriages" but were more likely to be cheating because they were looking for a little excitement in a "boring" union.

There are a handful of cheaters in a marriage that is not working.

The spouse does not have to be sexually involved with a different person to be regarded to be infidelity.

Women and men alike believe that cheating on non-sexual partners is as destructive as relationships that involve sexual activity. "Emotional connection" is more likely to result in tension in marriages since it's more than the sex aspect and also because there are emotional issues that are involved. An individual's wife or partner can be kinder when their spouse has cheated on an unrelated person than with a person they've known. "Sexting" and cyber relationships can also be considered cheating. If one is in the intent of keeping relationships that are not the same as those is with their spouse, they're already in the process of cheating.

Men are more likely to be attracted by women who are not their wives.

Many men believe that sexing with other women is acceptable. Many believe it's not cheating, but the majority of women believe that if the husbands of their partners kiss and they're already being cheated by him.

• Women have a higher likelihood transform casual relationships into genuine friendships.

When wives have a relationship to men who are not their husbands, they're more likely to stay in this relationship over the long term. Men are more into the random-kind-of-sex-and-relationship thing. Men tend to cheat when there were opportunities to indulge in it. This is not the case for women but. Most women do it because they are able to locate men who would give them the attention they would like their husbands to show the attention they deserved.

Women and men are stricken with guilt when they commit an infraction.

The guilt of men is greater whenever they are involved in sexual relations with someone else, whereas wives are more irritable, particularly when they discover that they are "falling" for someone else when they are married to their spouses.

Chapter 11: How do Affairs Begin?

If a spouse learns of that their partner has committed an infraction one of the first questions which is likely to pop up is when the incident began.

What is the first step to take when a spouse start to cheat? In some cases, they are unhappy with their relationship that stems from the spouse's inability to satisfy a vital psychological need. Women may require someone to talk to, and engage in the same discussions as that they did before having children. This is typically one reason why women are involved in affairs.

Many wives feel the requirement to stay emotionally attached with their husbands even after many years of marriage. Some men have, over the years married, are so busy with their work and children that they do not have the time to devote themselves to wife.

If her husband isn't able to meet that desire and she is looking for the answer outside of their relationship. Even though a husband can show that he is concerned about and loves his wife in a variety of ways, he isn't doing the same in a manner that the wife expects to. When there's a need that she needs and the husband isn't able to meet, she is more prone to being involved in an affair.

If she comes across someone she believes to share feelings of emotional intimacy to, it is an excellent chance for her to be drawn towards that person and have dating him due to a desire that did not get satisfied by her husband.

Sometime, relationships start in the most bizarre ways. It is common to hear of a husband being drawn to a former friend as a result of a moment when it was a moment of passion and they realized their desire.

Initial Attraction

When spouses fall in love by a different person, they must ensure that they get it nipped before it gets out of hand. In the above example in the event that a spouse believes that she has something that her husband isn't able to satisfy then the most sensible way to address it is to speak to her about the issue. A lot of marital issues could be resolved if each partner would discuss them. Instead of fostering the feelings of attraction for another instead, why not tackle the issue rather than inventing a new one?

The husband could not know how the wife is feeling and would be unable to find out if she decides to let go of it and choose not to discuss the issue.

People They Know

Like I said, affairs tend to be with those who a person knows for some time for example, co-workers or friends. Most likely because they're the people are spending time with, and are those they typically have a chat in the evenings after their work.

Cyber Relationship

Nowadays, there is a trend towards cyber relationships. It is among the dangers of being connected via the web. If a woman finds herself engaging in a conversation to a guy she's has met on the internet, she starts to share her feelings. If she's not cautious enough it is possible that she will fall in love with people she has met on online channels.

Honesty

If a wife is unhappy with something her husband not doing ought to speak up instead of searching at the outside world for ways to improve the marriage.

Chapter 12: How Affairs Should End?

There are three components of stopping an affair. The first step is that the spouse who has been cheating must disclose the indiscretion to their partner. Next step is to stop communication with the partner. Finally, ending your relationship with your lover will not be enough. You need to endure the process of healing the damaged relationship.

Though most marriages end either in separation or divorce However, some marriages remain intact and endure happily after.

Stopping the Love Affair with the One You Love

There are some affairs that have one-night stands, however there are also those in which emotions are at play. The majority of affairs satisfy only a few of the needs for emotional support which aren't met by the marriage. This leaves other needs which are taken care of by the spouse. The truth is that the majority of affairs don't result in divorce, in the case of the spouse that is in the relationship. A cheating spouse is aware the needs only their spouse is able to meet, which is why the majority of affairs are seen as a security net, which meets whatever cannot be fulfilled in the marriage.

Things are supposed to be kept a Private

In light of the findings on how to determine the "real" nature of affairs It is quite clear that a spouse cheating wants the matter to remain hidden. This is not only because being exposed can cause a lot of stress, however they want that the affair continue the duration of time that their requirements cannot be met within the relationship. It is a fact that many people don't realize is that cheating spouses generally don't really wish to end their relationship, but rather seek out a partner who can meet their needs, which do not meet the requirements of the marriage. The discovery of their affairs will be the final part of their "solution" to their marital difficulties.

Affair Running its Course

There's a moment when almost all relationships the spouse who is cheating would recognize that they have strayed from their course. Some would be able to see that it was not an ideal idea to begin an affair at all. Some cases are where lovers are who ends the relationship after determining that the spouse cheating is in no way living up expectations. There are instances when the cheating spouse is the one to end the relationship citing the death significance the affair brought to them or their.

Some relationships are peaceful, with two people agree to stop the relationship. There are also instances when lovers may not like the decision of the cheating spouse to stop the relationship, this could lead him or her to take extreme measures to scold the spouse cheating and cause a myriad of trouble. However, these situations are extremely uncommon since the majority of relationships conclude as calmly as they started.

The majority of the time the time, such affairs do not get discovered by the spouse even if the children are born as a result of the affair. It is the same in the case of wives who cheat (where there is a situation where the "victimized husband" is not conscious that he has the child who isn't his).

What are the Signs of an Affair?

If you confront them (with the evidence) with evidence, cheating spouses is likely to deny any involvement. It is nearly impossible to discover your partner and their lover on the same bed There are plenty different ways to spot the ongoing sins.

To allow the spouse who is in a bad mood to carry on the relationship without being caught the two lives of the couple have been created. One for the spouse and the other for the love of their life. There's some dishonesty necessary for both. But it is a major lie for the spouse.

The most important indicators of an affair is an unfaithful spouse's apparent inability to let the second person's life examined. A spouse's reluctance to discuss what transpired during their work day is an obvious sign there is something wrong. The most frequent ways to defend a cheating spouse is to show shock and displeasure when asked. The cheater will turn the tables, making the spouse feel ashamed for insecure and having too many questions.

A situation where a spouse is not involved could lead to an affair. Anything that restricts the partner from the same place for a night can be a clear invitation for an affair. An employee of the opposite gender who is accompanying the spouse on business trips should be a red flag.

Are you required to disclose your personal details?

There are a few indications of an infidelity between a couple However, there are few cheating spouses that have the courage to talk with their spouses regarding their lives without ever being challenged. In the majority of cases the guilt causes a spouse to open to their spouse about an alleged indiscretion. The guilt usually starts from the moment they first have sexual relations and continues to grow as one false accusation becomes a lie after another. It is common for depression to show up at moments when, in despair, when the cheating partner is forced to resort towards "honesty" as the last option to escape the mess that they caused.

The majority of marriage counselors believe that honesty can be a part of a solution for cheating. It can be difficult to reveal the truth for the unaware spouse, however this is the initial step toward reconciliation.

Many spouses who have been unfaithful are aware the fact that an affair is not a good thing and that one of the main reasons of lying is to shield their partner from suffering emotional trauma. They are aware the act they committed was not right and they do not want to "hurt" their spouse.

But, those who advocate for truth believe otherwise. Although it can be difficult to be, honesty is among crucial elements to the successfulness of marriage. Keeping the fact that there are infidelity (even when they've been already been dissolved) is a way to make marriages untrue, which can hinder the intimacy and emotional connection.

Honesty doesn't cause any pain but the incident is what causes the pain. Being honest is simply speaking the truth to an uninformed "victim".

The spouse who is cheating shouldn't think that the other partner isn't able to handle the reality. The cheater is being unprofessional and manipulative.

There is a possibility after the discovery that you have an affair your partner is less likely to trust you However, this loss of trust won't cause harm to your relationship, rather it's the absence of security and love that destroys it.

Stop communicating and seeing your Lover

When an affair is exposed the spouse who was the victim is shocked and their first reaction is fear, but quickly is followed by anger. The result could be divorce or, if it gets worse, even murder. However, after a certain period of time the majority of couples consider seeking to save their marriage.

The cheating spouse will try to bargain even however, he or she may not in a position negotiate, but attempts to do it regardless. The spouse who is not faithful will usually attempt to avoid having any contact with his or her spouse and attempt to convince the spouse who was victimized that it was only sexual.

At first, the injured spouse may want to see a total end to communication with her lover for the rest of their lives. In some cases, this could mean moving residences or even to a new place.

Although this could be a smart move but it's crucial to determine the primary source of the problem. in the case of the desire to have sex or a need to feel connected emotionally, no regardless of where you reside it is likely to present the chance to cheat. Even moving to a new area, should the opportunity arises an unfaithful spouse could remain enticed to give to.

Stopping the relationship and stopping all communications is important. However, the pledge of the cheating spouse to the other is vital, as is the commitment of not repeating this again, and addressing the root of the marriage issue.

Chapter 13: Restoring the Marriage

If an affair gets exposed when you as well as your partner decide to re-start the relationship What do you do to restore your union? In this post we will show you what each party can do to make new efforts to restore the relationship.

It's crucial to be aware that many extramarital affairs don't result in separation or divorce. If the issues which led to the incident are sorted out, both partners will not be in a position to continue. Although the matter was over, the main challenges to recovery are the emotions that have been caused by the incident.

The ideal scenario is that the spouse who has been unfaithful is expected to completely divorce from their partner and work to rebuild the relationship.

Recovery isn't an easy walk as there's still a sense of resentment, betrayal and anger. What is the best way to have the marriage that was strained back?

It's a normal feeling that spouses who have been unfaithful be regretful. This is because it's typical for the spouse who was victimized to believe that the incident was not their fault. Therefore, once the relationship is over and the couple begin to rebuild the relationship, neither would like to assume the blame. Each party tends to view the other as self-centered. They both believe it's each other's fault they're having issues in their relationship.

Talking it out

One of the best ways to start getting things settled is to get each of the parties to speak. In spite of the events that have been revealed, when the situation is exposed and concluded Therapists advise each spouse to accept their own apology to one another. the spouse who was infidelity is expected to apologize for his or her actions as well as the one who has been victimized must apologize for failing to fulfill the crucial "emotional needs" that were stated at the start of marriage.

Apologizing is a crucial component of the healing and rebuilding process, because firstly, it can help bring the matter under control. After an apology has been made and the couple has begun taking steps forward to get past the issue as well as any other missteps that were made during the course of their wedding. It's time to begin new.

The separation from the love of your life is a significant step and is followed by sincerely apologizing What happens after? Rebuilding the relationship must be the result of a joint effort by both sides. Once both parties have passed the apology stage then it is evident that they both have the ability to compromise and both are committed to fixing their relationship.

For a successful restoration of the marriage following an incident, couples must take to rest the "weapons". Each of them must work together not to resort to violence, the ill-treatment of others, causing anger or demanding unreasonable demands. Every one of them must do the best they can, no matter what is necessary, to build a stronger marriage and ensure that the marriage is working for the two of them.

When they've ensured the safety of each other They are now ready to start learning about how they can meet the needs of their spouses emotionally. The process of rebuilding their marriage will require both partners to be willing not to engage in actions which could hurt their partner.

If they are able to come to an objective that is common to the two parties can build their relationship. Once they have set the scene to have a secure discussion, it is imperative that the disagreement be addressed. Each party should attempt to respect and comprehend the other when they share their viewpoints and views in the issues. If they do not are able to discuss issues of "conflict" and the marital issues, their marriage will not be as successful as they would like it to.

Both parties must agree to working together on the resolution of conflicts and mutual respect and understanding are essential for success.

The presentation of possible solutions is the final step towards making the marriage work. Both parties must share their individual solutions for the issue without being criticised. One of the best ways to determine an acceptable resolution is to talk with one another out.

The final step is important because both parties need to be energized to make the solution effective. The resolution is not likely to be successful for success if one person is eager to tackle the issue but the other party isn't.

The key for resolving marital disputes and issues is for both partners put in a collective effort to commit and collaborate to achieve success.

Chapter 14: Overcoming Resentment

If you're the one who's been victimized by your spouse, you'll experience feelings of resentment and anger. Feeling abandoned, neglected and extremely angry following realizing that your spouse has an affair. The spouse who is cheating knows the damage an act of infidelity can cause to an innocent spouse. Continuedly having the affair shows complete disregard for the feelings of an innocent spouse.

The first response of the spouse who was cheated on will be to request divorce, as most have a difficult time with an "normal relationship" after being victimized by someone "you promised to have and to hold, till death do you part". Feeling resentful is most likely an exaggeration of how one can feel every time you contemplate what happened to the cheating spouse has done.

As you've probably heard from now on, the majority of relationships don't end with divorce or separation. The majority of couples attempt to sort things through and come to a compromise with each other, and many people succeed in getting things back in order and coming out more unified. It's true that, even after working it out, you're in the end one human being that was injured in the first place. And even the time you managed to overcome that "crisis", the feelings of anger will never go away and sometimes reappear.

Do you ever forget?

Although the memories of the event and everything related to it will not disappear, the feeling of resentment are able to be overcome. Many marriage counselors believe that marriages are able to thrive following infidelity.

171

Then you forget the incident by making fresh memories as two people. It's normal to be thinking about your affair every time you get intimate with your partner, that was not trustworthy. When you're brought back to it and you are afflicted with the same hurt and relive the pain. It is important to recognize that those feelings are likely to disappear over time, as long as you don't create any further connections to it.

The process of forgetting is one that takes time that can be a source of anger and resentment. and anger form one of the steps. The process requires you to be aware of every emotion that goes along with it. There is no way to get around it. If you're not capable of manage your emotions and feelings, you'll never confront the root of the issue.

Leave Everything in the Past

If you're hoping to totally live your life as a couple you must learn to let go and put all of the memories from your past. If you are clinging to the memories and the longer it takes to get over resentment since emotions of irritation are tied to those past memories. It may be difficult initially, if you don't remember that painful moment and feel resentment, those feelings are eventually lost with it.

Resolving Past Issues

In order to resolve any past issues it is best to address the issues one by one then bring a solution to the table then proceed. There is no way to resolve any issue that isn't resolved regardless of having discussed regarding them and put those questions to bed. The only way to ensure that reconciliation will be carried out is when both parties agree to it.

Focus on the Present and the Future

The past has passed and you must give it up today. It is time to turn your focus towards the present and the near future as you are able to take action to create great memories. Avoid spending your moment looking back on your past and all of negative events that occurred and you can't make any changes in the future. Only look back to the past to reflect on the lessons that you learned. But don't dwell about them for too long. Learn from the experience however, forget all that is happening, and get started again.

Avoid using Resentment to punish your spouse

The most frequent errors that spouses who are abused commit is to use resentment as a way to control and punish the partner who has been unfaithful. It is an effective strategy to obtain the things you desire from a person who committed a blunder and has hurt you previously. If this occurs it is clear that the incident is not any longer the problem, it is the spouse who was victimized utilizes the situation to get the upper hand within the new relationship. The spouse that is victimized wants to take control of the marriage, and is using the past mistakes to achieve this objective.

Never Mention the Affair Ever Again

If you've had a discussion about the issues and reached a conclusion for marital disputes The best thing you can be sure not to revisit them. If one person is prone to bringing up their mistakes from the past each when there's a dispute this will make discussions unpleasant, and won't help solve any issues.

Quit Obsessive Thinking

Some people have, when they discover that someone made an error that has caused them pain, are prone to be prone to thinking about the error repeatedly. The feeling is of fear that other people will make the same mistake, and will suffer the pain and anger repeatedly. If you keep worrying about this, the more enthralled you get, and the more anxious you'll become. There is no way to truly move on to your spouse if continue to think about another chance to repeat what's been averted. Relax and believe that your partner is ready to let go of their past to start making new memories with them.

Chapter 15: Surviving Infidelity

The marriage you have is still able to survive the ravages of infidelity. It may be difficult to heal and require a lot of work and pain, however when both partners are dedicated to making the marriage stronger you can do it. Stopping the affair is only an aspect of it, but getting it done and building trust is another. The person who has been cheated on must learn to let go of the anger and bitterness that this affair brought and get on with her life.

If you agree to a deal to each other, here are the 15 most effective ways to survive an affair in building a stronger, more unified relationship.

For the Unfaithful Spouse

1. Stop the romance. The act of putting an end to the relationship also implies a cessation of all communications with the

person you love, immediate. Accept to end the secret so that there is the feeling of security those who were betrayed by their spouse. Stopping the relationship doesn't just indicate that you can't take dates with your lover and also the end of sexual activity. Also, it means stopping any phone calls, texts messages, as well as other kinds of messages.

If you're within the same workplace interactions should be strictly professional and you should inform your spouse of on what is happening in the office. Lunches at private parties are a no-no as are private meeting rooms for business.

2. Answer all questions. Many marriage counselors agree that there's a greater probability of healing for the couple in the aftermath of an affair, if the spouse who is not faithful provides all

information required by the spouse who has been retreated. Be honest with your spouse will help to build an emotional bond and peace is effortlessly. The act of discussing your relationship assists your spouse in being able to get rid of the grief and hurt. In refusing to talk about the affair, you cover up the hurt, but it lingers. Once you're able to speak about the event with no pain, healing becomes more easily.

The willingness of you to be totally transparent can assist your spouse who has been cheated to trust the person who betrayed them. An unfaithful spouse must not keep quiet and avoid telling secrets for long. If you don't leave any step unturned, it'll help the wife who was betrayed to understand the situation and be able to move on.

3. Be compassionate No matter the situation. The advice of marriage counselors is that the most reliable indicator of whether the marriage will survive an affair is the degree of understanding shown by an not-faithful partner when the liar spouse gets too emotional as a result of the grief and emotional trauma caused from the act of infidelity. Emotional feelings shouldn't be brushed aside and one should avoid interpreting the minor emotional breakdowns as a way to alter the relationships. It is a real feeling and you ought to be able to understand those feelings.

4. Do not stop listening and talking throughout the time you can. The rehabilitation process doesn't have shortcuts. A couple, and especially the spouse who has been cheated on, needs to undergo the procedure and shouldn't

be forced upon any person. Continue to talk and keep looking. Always be prepared to respond to the questions. There's no end date to healing. it could take months to a year or many years before the spouse that was betrayed is completely healed. It is not a time to indulge in guilt or anger during the process of healing.

5. Take responsibility for your error. Relying on your spouse's personal infidelity won't help rebuild your relationship. Be honest and take responsibility in apologizing for your error. Acknowledge your mistake and then make the commitment not to repeat the same thing ever again. Don't justify the act of infidelity with arguments about the inadequacies of your spouse. Although these arguments may be accurate and you may have a spouse responsible for the actions you've

done, the fact is that it's nonetheless your fault. In the event that you choose to engage in an affair with someone else, it's because you did not take care of the marital problems as you should had: namely, to address what is the cause of the problem.

An affair can be described as trying to escape your marital issues. Some people say that they decided to get involved as you did not want to cause harm to your spouse by telling them that there was something not right in the union.

This is probably due to pride that you were hesitant to acknowledge that there was something amiss, and therefore rather than "hurting" him or her by revealing the problem, you continued with your affair. "The "solution" is more hurtful than telling your partner there's a crack within the union.

6. You shouldn't be expecting to receive forgiveness immediately. The person you love is suffering from immense pain and is in states of shock.

You shouldn't be expecting to receive forgiveness too quickly as your spouse will have to face emotions like anger, tears as well as a great deal of hurt. Your only option to overcome it is for your spouse go through the experience. Don't get in a defensive mood if she is angry; since you brought up the relationship when you made the decision to continue with your affair.

Let your partner be able to forgive you. As time passes you must work to show your spouse how they is able to trust you. Demonstrate that you still can be reliable. It is important to demonstrate to your client you're willing to make this work.

For the Betrayed Spouse

You can understand why you are looking to get angry with your partner. There is no doubt that you want to learn everything there is regarding the situation. If you've agreed to repair your marriage, you're hoping for the secret to be dissolved. Following steps can assist to go through healing to repair the marriage and get on with your life.